A story to introduce the 'William Tell' Overture

William
THE CRACK SHOT KID

Editor: Robin Norman
Illustrations: Paul Selvey
Design and Layout: John Good Holbrook
Cd recording issued under license from Sanctuary Records Group Ltd.

Reproducing this book in any form is illegal and forbidden by the Copyright, Designs and Patents Act 1988

IMP
International
MUSIC
Publications

© International Music Publications Limited Griffin House 161 Hammersmith Road London W6 8BS England
Published 2004

Introducing Classical Music Through Stories
A Triple Resource
MUSIC • LITERACY • ART

As a specialist art teacher I found there were so many possibilities to explore an aspect of art such as colour in an unusual approach, and the project based on Crazy Alien Ball fitted very neatly into the art curriculum.

I decided not to show the children the illustrations at first, but asked them to build pictures in their minds. They were full of exciting ideas and were totally absorbed in their pictures as the music played in a loop after the initial story reading.

I was so inspired by this I have decided to do a lengthier project with next year's Year 4, introducing an IT element. Scanning in images and experimenting with colour techniques would be a valuable progression, as would using lettering programmes to work with the illustrations. Another interesting development could be the creation of a class collage using cut out images assembled against an atmospheric background. Wonderful!

Jan Fleming, Specialist Art Teacher, Somerhill, Tonbridge

The Year 3 class were enchanted by the combination of music, text and illustrations in William the Crack Shot Kid, and were very quickly involved in the written task I set them. They loved writing their own versions of the story to fit the music and I was particularly impressed by the inspired work produced by children with learning difficulties. Ideas came, sentences flowed and stories evolved, and the oil pastel illustrations the children did were an added bonus. The activity extended to a whole day and the session finished with the class reading each other their stories as the music was played yet again, followed by requests to do the same task the next day!

Ann Bourne, Year 3 Generalist Teacher, Bedgebury Junior School

---

THE 6 TITLES OF STORIES IN THE SERIES, AND THE MUSIC ON WHICH THEY ARE BASED

Set One

WASP ALERT IN MINIBUG BONANZALAND
Overture:The Wasps
by Ralph Vaughan Williams
British
1872 - 1958

THE INCREDIBLE SPINNING WHEEL
Omphale's Spinning Wheel
by Camille Saint-Saëns
French
1835 - 1921

———————•———————

Set Two

WILLIAM THE CRACK SHOT KID
Overture: William Tell
by Gioacchino Rossini
Italian
1792 - 1868

THE CRAZY ALIEN BALL
A Night on Bare Mountain
by Modest Mussorgsky
Russian
1839 - 1881

———————•———————

Set Three

BILLY BRIGGS, BIG ON SKATES
The Moldau from 'Ma Vlast'
by Frederick Smetana
Czech
1824 - 1884

JUPITER COVE
Jupiter from 'The Planets Suite'
by Gustav Holst
British
1874 - 1934

———————•———————

ABOUT THE BOOK

The books are designed to be used as part of your scheme of work for music, literacy and art and will particularly help generalists, as they are straight forward, interesting and fun to use.

If you ask children what they think of classical music they often say 'It's boring.' That's an understandable reaction. Classical music doesn't have the 'immediacy' of pop, rock, rap etc. It lacks a constant even beat, often lacks lyrics and is usually longer than the average pop song.

However pieces such as *The Sorcerer's Apprentice* usually prove very popular with young children. Why? Because they have strong contrasting dynamics, are very descriptive, and best of all, they have a story. It is the story, particularly when combined with illustrations, that is the instant attraction.

Many pieces of classical music either do not have a story at all, or have an inappropriate one – too old, too complicated, too scary or simply too uninteresting. This series uses original stories written specifically for young children and inspired by short interesting pieces of music from a variety of different cultures. Although the stories are original, they bear some association with the title and flavour of the music.

●

HOW TO USE THIS BOOK

1. AS A MUSIC RESOURCE

Simply read the story to the class, showing the pictures on the way, with the music playing at the same time. It tells you in the story when to put on the CD. Make sure you play the music loudly enough for it to be clearly heard, but not so loud that it overpowers your voice. It is a good idea to have the remote control on hand so you can adjust the volume control when necessary! Tell the children beforehand that you want them to be silent throughout the story.

You need to read the story so it 'matches' the music. For this reason, time indications (e.g. 3:42) have been included on the page and you will need to keep an eye on the counter of the CD player, in order to pace your reading of each section of text. The story has been flexibly designed to enhance the piece of music. This means that sometimes the children will simply be listening to the music, while looking at the illustration which you are holding up. Their imaginations will be working away, because they are in effect 'suspended' within the story. Try it out beforehand so you have a feel for how the story fits the music. Remember the story is only the vehicle for capturing the children's attention. It is important that it doesn't dominate to such an extent that the music becomes lost in the background, secondary to the story.

After listening you might like to talk about the contrasts in the music. For example loud/quiet, fast/slow, high/low and smooth/bouncy. Discuss the feelings the music evoked; such as fear, calm, wonder or amazement. In your discussion, use descriptive words – scary, peaceful, gentle, mysterious, tense, magical. All this is valuable work, focusing the children on the style, mood and atmosphere of the music.

The next stage is to play the music *without* reading the story. Just show the pictures, pausing for as long as you feel on each illustration so they can mentally follow the story through the pictures.

And finally listen to the music without any verbal or visual aids at all. Now the children's imaginations are 'buzzing' they will enjoy the music in its own right a great deal more than they would have done, had they heard it without the benefit of the story the first time round.

2. AS A LITERACY RESOURCE

It is usual for creative writing to be inspired by a story, a picture, an illustration, an experience or a poem. With this resource the music adds a further starting point, as well as an additional dimension to the story. There are three ways in which to use the resource:-

1) Read the story without the music, showing the pictures, and get the children to evolve their own stories based on the same characters.

2) Use the music only, as a brainstorming exercise for the whole class, to inspire poetry or a piece of creative writing.

3) Use the story in conjunction with the music (see 'HOW TO USE THE BOOK AS A MUSIC RESOURCE') to show how the two media interact. This might stimulate poetry or a piece of creative/imaginative writing.

3. AS AN ART RESOURCE

This resource can be used in three distinctive ways, either individually or worked together to form a project of half a term or a term's duration.

The first stage is to give children the opportunity to look at the work of illustrative artists, analysing the media and examining the various techniques used, as well as considering how the text and illustration are incorporated on the page. This is an important part of the art design section of the National Curriculum.

The second stage is for the children to engage with the music and the story, absorbing the atmospheres and moods evoked by the storyline, then to develop their own ideas using materials related to illustrations they have seen.

The final stage is to use I.T. If facilities permit, the children should learn how to scan their pictures into *Publisher*, and then to apply text to the page so that the best possible layout is achieved.

About the 'William Tell' Overture by Rossini (1792-1868)

Rossini is an Italian composer, he lived from 1792 to 1868. *William Tell* is the last of Rossini's thirty-six operas. It is not performed as an opera these days, but the overture (the instrumental opening to an opera) is frequently heard. The famous, galloping tune, is only a small part of this beautiful overture, which is a wonderful example of picture music and is sometimes called *'A Little Symphony of the Mountains'*.

The opera itself is set in the early 14th century and reflects the oppressive Austrian domination of Switzerland by the cruel governor Gessler. It tells the story of how William Tell was brave enough to defy Gessler to help his Swiss compatriots. On one occasion, Gessler placed his cap on a pole in a market square and ordered the Swiss citizens to bow to it as a symbol of their respect. William Tell and his little son passed by without bowing.

Furious at being disobeyed, Gessler captured Tell and ordered him to shoot an arrow with his crossbow at an apple placed on his son's head. Tell split the apple in half, but Gessler still arrested him. Tell escaped, tracked down Gessler and shot an arrow through his heart. This gave his countrymen the confidence to band with him and drive out the Austrian invaders, so Switzerland became free once more.

To keep something of the flavour of this story (without the blood and gore!) I have retained the name of William for the hero and kept the symbol of the apple. The opening of the music is slow and peaceful, then there is a more turbulent passage, which dies away. After that you will hear the *cor anglais* (English horn) play an imitation of the Swiss cattle call (which would have been played in the Alps on an alphorn, a long, curved, wooden horn. This is followed by a calm melody and then a sudden trumpet call precedes the lively familiar music which brings the overture to a close.

Now enjoy the story!

William kept his eye on the old tin. It was balanced on the lowest branch of the lightning tree which stood in the far corner of his garden. Carefully he drew back the elastic band. The pebble shot out of his catapult and seered through the air. Ping! The tin flew off the branch.

"Wow!" breathed Chris. "Brilliant shot!"

"William!" came his mum's voice. "Come in now. It's beginning to get dark."

"Go quick!" William whispered to his friend, Chris. "Before she sees you!"

And as Chris scrambled off through the gap in the fence, William hurried indoors.

CD ON

His mum was still standing by the kitchen window.
"Poor old apple tree!" she said quietly.

William's dad spoke in a grave voice.

"Forget about the tree.
It's been struck by lightning
and there's nothing anyone
can do to save it now."'

00:28

Up in his bedroom, William looked out of the window. In the gloom he could just make out the lightning tree, dark and charred at the bottom of the garden, its craggy branches bent and gnarled like giant witches' fingers. Some of them pointed over the fence into Chris's garden, and the ones at the back dropped brittle twigs on to Mrs Green's neat lawn.

01:09

Mrs Green's cat, Greg, had fallen ill the
very day lightning struck the tree. Poor old
Greg. He lay flopped out on the sitting
room window sill. When it was day time,
William could just make out the tufts and
clumps of his scrawny form.

01:39

The day after the tree was struck, William had shot a pebble from his catapult straight through next door's kitchen window.

Chris's dad had gone mad and said that Chris and William weren't to play together any more.

So since then the two boys had to meet in secret.

02:13

"All this illness and sadness and crossness,"
William's mum kept saying.

"Fancy not being friends with your
neighbours."

Then she would shake her head.

"And no more apples from the poor
old tree, ever again."

02:39

But that night, as William stared out of his bedroom window, he got a shock.

"What! I don't believe it! It can't be!"

It was difficult to tell in the half light but...what was that hanging from the very top branch of the tree?

William gasped.

How could an apple have grown on a dead tree?

03:24

The next morning, the moment it was light,
William rushed outside and stood beneath
the lightning tree.

His eyes widened as he looked up.

There was no doubt about it now.

Above him hung a mottled
green and red gleaming apple.

03:50

"What are you looking at?" said Chris, from his side of the fence.

He followed William's gaze and when he saw the apple, started yelling and pointing.

"Dad! Come here! There's an apple on the lightning tree!"

04:10

Chris's dad came running out of the house at the same time as William's mum and dad.

04:23

From her sitting room window, Mrs Green saw the little crowd standing round the old lightning tree.

Whatever was going on?

04:39

She slipped out of the back door and hurried down to see.

04:50

"It's a lucky charm!" she breathed, as she gazed up at the apple, eyes gleaming.

"And look! It's on the branch that's hanging over *my* garden!

"This tree belongs to us!" said William's dad coldly. "If there's good luck to be had, it should be ours!"

Chris's dad spoke in a low voice. "It was *my* grandfather who planted the tree in the first place."

05:28

William couldn't believe what he was hearing. The adults were arguing over an apple.

One little apple and they'd all gone mad.

05:54

No-one even noticed as he crept back inside the house, and went up to his room.

There, he stood at the open window, and watched and listened.

06:11

Even Chris was joining in with the argument, saying he was going to climb up the tree and get the apple for himself, because *he* deserved the luck.

His dad shook his head. "That tree'll break if you climb it. Look at it! Dry as string!"

06:47

If only there were more apples, thought William.
Then everyone could have a bit of the luck.

And that gave him an idea...

07:06

He picked up his piggy bank and emptied it out onto the bed.

Amongst the silver pieces lay a two pound coin.

7:29

William took the catapult from his bedside table and went back to the window.

Down below nobody noticed.

08:00

The next bit needed great concentration.

Carefully placing the coin in the catapult, William took aim.

08:24

Then he pulled the elastic back as far as it would go.

08:32

Ping! The coin cut through the air, gleaming and gold. Everyone gasped.

There was a sharp THWACK!

08:45

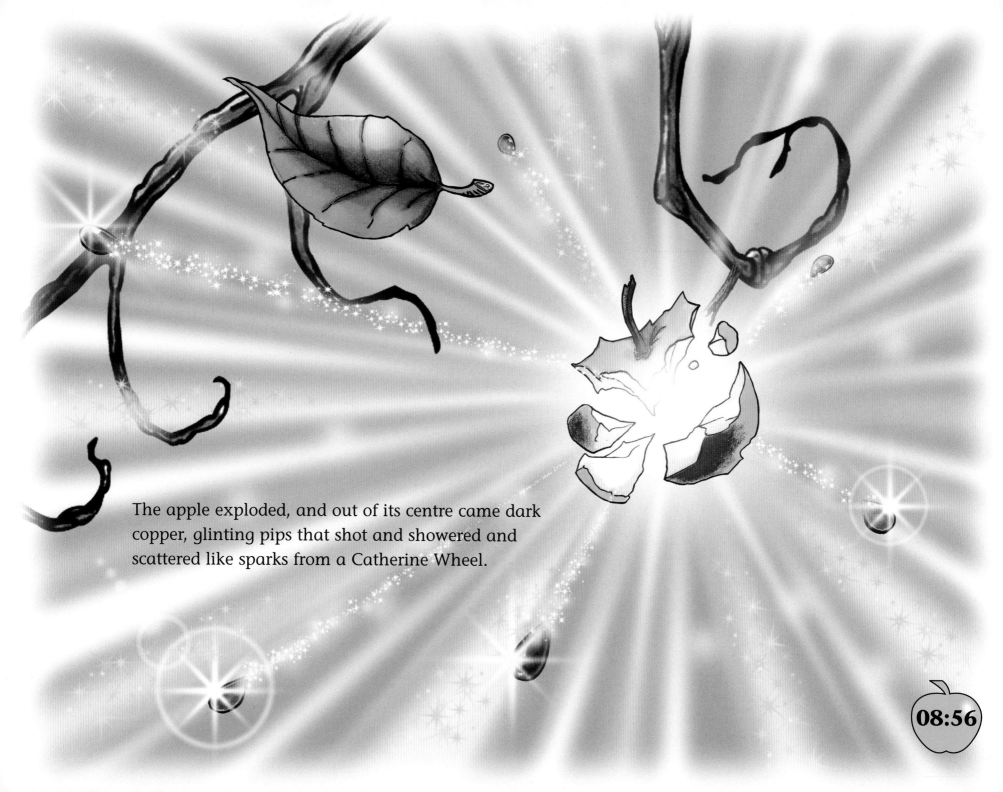

The apple exploded, and out of its centre came dark copper, glinting pips that shot and showered and scattered like sparks from a Catherine Wheel.

08:56

"Incredible! Amazing! Brilliant!" everyone cried as they stood wide-eyed under the golden shower.

09:08

Some of the neighbours heard the shouting and came hurrying to see what was happening.

"William's a crack shot! He's split the lucky apple!" cried Chris proudly. Then he stopped, and stared at the tree.

09:27

Gasps rose from the crowd.

Glittering streams of bright apple juice were trickling over the high branches, painting them gold.

09:38

Everywhere buzzed with news of the miracle tree.

09:47

More and more people came to look. They stared in amazement as the liquid fell in sparkling drops coating the lower branches.

10:05

In no time at all the journalists were out in force. **10:17**

As the cameras flashed, the glistening liquid rose up
and dissolved into thin air, and the frail dark branches
grew strong and supple as though touched by magic.

10:34

Then into the middle of the incredible scene stepped a beautiful sleek cat.

"It's Greg!" cried Mrs Green. "He's better!" 10:45

Everyone cheered. Even Chris's dad. "Your boy certainly is a crack shot with that catapult," he said to William's parents. 10:57

Also Available from IMP, these Great Schemes of Work for Specialist and Non-Specialist Teachers

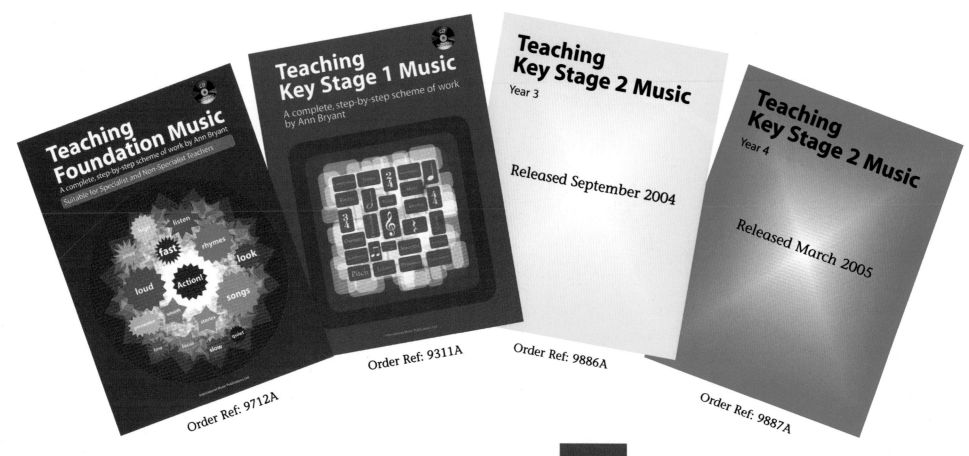

Teaching Foundation Music
A complete, step-by-step scheme of work by Ann Bryant
Suitable for Specialist and Non-Specialist Teachers
Order Ref: 9712A

Teaching Key Stage 1 Music
A complete, step-by-step scheme of work by Ann Bryant
Order Ref: 9311A

Teaching Key Stage 2 Music
Year 3
Released September 2004
Order Ref: 9886A

Teaching Key Stage 2 Music
Year 4
Released March 2005
Order Ref: 9887A

IMP, for all your Music at School needs.
www.music-at-school.co.uk

International Music Publications Ltd.
Griffin House, 161 Hammersmith Road, London, W6 8BS